Ceremonies and Celebrations

LIFE'S END

DENISE CHAPLIN AND
LYNNE BROADBENT

D1439260

W
HODDER
Wayland
an imprint of Hodder Children's Books

Ceremonies and Celebrations

LIFE'S END

Other titles in this series are:

BIRTHS • WEDDINGS • FEASTS AND FASTING

GROWING UP • PILGRIMAGES AND JOURNEYS

Produced for Hodder Wayland by
Roger Coote Publishing
Gissing's Farm, Fressingfield
Suffolk IP21 5SH, UK

Published in Great Britain in 2001 by Hodder Wayland, an imprint of
Hodder Children's Books

This edition published 2001

© Hodder Wayland 2001

Editor: Alex Edmonds
Designer: Katrina ffiske

Consultants:
Khadijah Knight is a teacher and consultant on multicultural education
and Islam. She is also the author of several children's books about Islam.
Marcus Braybrooke is a parish priest, lecturer and writer on interfaith
relations. He is joint President of the World Congress of Faiths.
Kanwaljit Kaur-Singh is a local authority inspector for education.
She has written many books on the Sikh tradition and appears on
television regularly.
Sharon Barron regularly visits schools to talk to children about Judaism.
She has written two books about Judaism for Hodder Wayland.
Meg St. Pierre is the Director of the Clear Vision Trust, a charitable
trust that aims to inform and educate about the teachings of Buddha.
VP Hemant Kanitkar is a retired teacher and author of many books
on Hinduism.

Picture acknowledgements
Circa Picture Library 22, 27; Hutchison Picture Library front cover
top left (Moser), front cover bottom left (J C Tordai), 16 (J Horner),
17 (M MacIntyre); Panos Pictures 5 (S Sprague), 23 (Jean Léo
Dugast), 24 (Jean Léo Dugast); Peter Sanders Picture Library 1 (J
Gulliver), 6, 19 (J Gulliver), 20 (J Gulliver), 21 (J Gulliver); Trip
front cover top right (H Rogers), front cover bottom right (H
Rogers), 4 (H Rogers), 7 (H Rogers), 8 (P Rauter), 9 (H Rogers), 10
(S Shapiro), 11 (I Genut), 12 (I Genut), 13 (H Rogers), 14 (H
Rogers), 15 (H Rogers), 18 (Ibrahim), 25 (R Morgan), 26 (H
Rogers), 27 (H Rogers), 28 (H Rogers), 29 (H Rogers).

A Catalogue record for this book is available from the British Library.

ISBN 0 7502 3308 7

Printed and bound in Italy by G. Canale & C.S.p.A., Turin

Hodder Children's Books
a division of Hodder Headline Limited
338 Euston Road, London NW1 3BH

CONTENTS

The Journey through Life

▲ Mourners often send flowers to a funeral as a last gift to the deceased. Because flowers don't last for long, they symbolize the fact that human life is short.

We all start our life as small babies and grow into adults. We continue to grow older and then at the end of our life, we die. That is the cycle of human life. Just as many religions have ceremonies and celebrations to mark the start of people's lives, so there are many different ceremonies to mark the end of them.

Throughout time people have asked questions about death, such as 'What happens to the person who has died?' and 'Is death really the end?' People have answered these questions in many different ways. The answer depends on what people believe. Some believe that death is the end of life and there is nothing after death. Others believe that their soul will be close to God, while some think that the soul will have another life in a new body.

Most faiths believe that when people die, they don't cease to exist completely. Although they may not be on Earth, their souls have gone to a better place, often described as heaven, or Paradise. Some religions believe that if someone has done bad deeds, his or her soul will not go directly to heaven and might go to hell, a place where people are punished for their sins. Some faiths believe in reincarnation. This is when a person's soul is reborn into a new body to live another life. What people believe affects the way in which they say goodbye to the person who has died and the celebrations that mark the end of life.

When someone dies, he or she often leaves behind many grieving friends and relatives. Some faiths see death as a time to be thankful for the person's life. They try to make funerals happy celebrations when lots of people get together to celebrate the life of the person who has died. Funerals will also be sad times for family and friends and occasions on which to reflect quietly on the life of the dead person. Most faiths have ceremonies to help the relatives accept their bereavement. These ceremonies bring family and friends together to grieve and support each other. This book looks at the six main faith traditions and the ceremonies and celebrations that they take part in when someone within their community dies.

Faith traditions celebrate both the beginning and the end of life. They welcome new babies into their faith, and say goodbye to those who die, with different ceremonies. ▼

The Christian Tradition

C hristians believe that Jesus' death on the first Good Friday, when he was crucified by the Romans, was not the end of his life. On Easter Sunday Christians celebrate their belief that Jesus rose from the dead. To Christians, this means that when they die, death will not be an end for them either. Christians believe that the special part of a person that makes them who they are, their soul or spirit, can go to have a new life with God.

Jesus was crucified on a cross. The cross has come to symbolize Christ's resurrection from the dead. ▼

Lent and Easter

Although Good Friday is a sad time, Easter Sunday is a celebration, because Christians believe that Jesus rose from the dead on that day. Christians see death as both sad and happy. They are sad that they will not see the deceased person again in this life, but they believe that they will meet again in a new life, after death. At a funeral Christians say goodbye until then and give thanks for the loved one's life. Before they die, some Christians want to say goodbye to their families and put right any misunderstandings. They may ask a priest to say prayers with them and they may want to confess things to that priest that they have done wrong. Christians believe that if they are really sorry, God will forgive them and their soul will go to be with God in heaven.

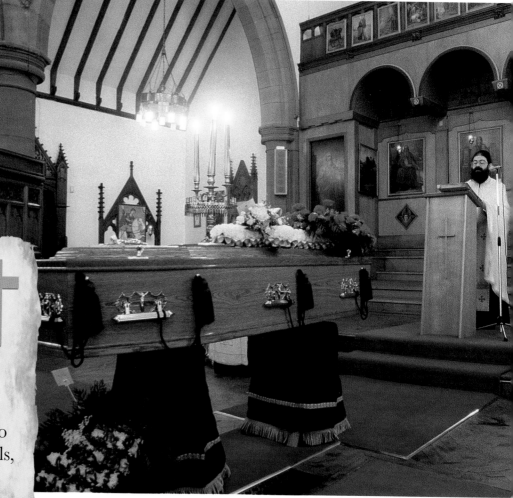

The coffin stands in the church during the funeral service so that relatives feel close to the dead person during the ceremony. ▶

Sacred text ✝

This text tells Christians how God sent Jesus to the world in order that he could teach them to be good and save their souls, so that they can go to heaven when they die.

'For God so loved the world that he gave his only Son, that whoever believes in Him should not perish but have eternal life. For God sent not his Son into the world to condemn the world; but that the world through him might be saved.'

The Bible: John 3 verse 16

Returning to the Earth

'Earth to Earth, ashes to ashes, dust to dust; in sure and certain hope of the resurrection to eternal life . . .' These words are said at most Christian funeral services. They remind Christians that God made everything and that when someone dies, his or her body returns to the Earth, which was used so the Bible says by God to create the first people (Adam and Eve). These words also remind Christians of their belief that after death they will be with God in heaven.

Saying goodbye

While some Christians believe that the dead should be buried, others prefer to cremate a dead person's body. Usually a funeral director, or undertaker organizes the funeral or the cremation for the family. If the person is buried, he or she may have a grave with a headstone. When someone is cremated, the ashes may be buried in a special garden of remembrance, or they may be scattered in a place that was special to the deceased.

The dead person's body is placed in a coffin. Sometimes family and friends like to visit the body in a Chapel of Rest at the undertaker's premises or at home before the funeral, to pray for the dead person and those who love them. Sometimes, family and friends sit by the corpse and watch over it for the last few hours before the burial.

Sometimes the coffin is carried on its last journey, to the cemetery, by male friends and members of the family. ▼

◄ *The priest leads prayers at the graveside and oversees the burial of the coffin.*

The funeral service

Before the burial or cremation, a funeral service, led by a priest, is held – usually in a church or chapel. People pray and read from the Bible to remind them of what Jesus said about death. Relatives and friends may talk about the person who has died, sharing memories, and the music and hymns that are chosen may have been favourites of the deceased.

People may wear dark clothes or black armbands when someone has died, particularly at the funeral. Dark colours show respect for the dead and they show that the bereaved are sad. People often send flowers to a funeral. They may be made into shapes using wire frames – round shapes are called wreaths. Sometimes words are spelt out in flowers, such as the name of the dead person. Flowers remind people that life is short and sweet. In recent times, instead of sending flowers, people have preferred to give money to a favourite charity of the person who has died. Friends and family often send cards of sympathy and write letters to the next of kin, and a priest may call round to offer support.

Paul's story

'My name is Paul, I am an English Jamaican. I was in Jamaica when my cousin Martin died. In the past a funeral happened the day after someone died but now, with families spread around the world, it happens as soon as families can get together. We had a special party – a wake – all night before the funeral for friends and neighbours to come and eat, share happy memories and sing hymns with us. The next day we went to the church for the funeral service. The coffin was open so everyone could see Martin and say goodbye. In the past people dressed in black or white for a funeral but these days many people dress in colourful clothes. We carried the coffin to its grave. A band played as we filled the grave, singing hymns while we worked. Although it was a sad occasion, everybody tried to be happy.'

The Jewish Tradition

▲ *A year after the funeral, a simple headstone is placed on the grave.*

Jews believe that death is a natural part of life. They believe that everyone lives just once on this Earth and then dies. Many traditional Jews believe that the soul is immortal. If a Jewish woman or man is very ill or old and about to die, he or she tries to ask God to forgive any wrongs committed throughout his or her life. Then he or she may recite the *Shema*, an important prayer that shows that the person believes in one God and is a devout Jew.

Sacred text

The *Shema* begins with these words which are said to show devotion to God.

'Hear, O Israel,
the Lord is our God,
the Lord is One.
And you shall love the Lord
your God
with all your heart, with all your
soul, and with all
your might.'

From the *Shema*.

When the person dies, the body is washed and wrapped in a simple white shroud. If the person was a man, then his prayer shawl, called a *tallit*, is placed around his body. The fringes or *tzizit* on the four corners of the prayer shawl, which are there to remind Jews of the Commandments a Jew must follow, are cut off as the man no longer has to remember these Commandments. Most Jews are buried because traditionally cremation was forbidden. The coffin is plain and made from simple wood. Everyone, rich or poor, has the same type of coffin. A simple coffin shows that in death everyone is equal before God. A lighted candle is put by the head of the dead person as he or she lies in their coffin and someone remains with the body constantly until the funeral can take place.

The funeral

The funeral is held as soon as possible after the person has died. Occasionally the funeral is held on the day of death, but sometimes the funeral is delayed to give relatives that live a long way away a chance to travel. A rabbi leads some prayers in the home before the burial. The prayers ask God to support the relatives and make them strong enough to cope with the loss. They also ask God to remember the goodness of the person who has died and allow him or her to rest in peace.

At the burial, psalms are recited over the coffin and then a eulogy (a speech that praises someone) is spoken by the rabbi, a family member or friend of the deceased. This is a chance to say something personal about the person who has died and to say goodbye to him or her. Then a memorial prayer is said and the coffin is lowered into the ground. Relatives throw soil onto the coffin in its grave as Psalm 91 is repeated. This Psalm describes how God protects all of his people and loves them and leads them to salvation. Jews don't often have flowers at a funeral. They prefer to give the money to charity on behalf of the dead person.

▲ *This picture shows details from a book, the* Sefer Haminhagim, *containing a blessing that is often said at Jewish funerals.*

Special rituals

The rituals that Jews follow when someone dies, help family and friends to express their sadness and accept their loss. For seven days after the funeral, the family stays at home to mourn the dead person. They will not prepare any food or wear leather shoes and the men will not shave. These are signs that normal life is suspended. Usually, the family sit on low stools rather than on chairs – this time is sometimes called 'sitting *Shiva*'. *Shiva* means 'seven', for the seven days of mourning. Mourners will often have items of clothing torn as a sign of their grief.

During this time friends will come to visit the family and bring food for them to eat.

A service is held in the house each day, usually in the evening, and the mourner's prayer, the *kaddish*, is recited. The *kaddish* reminds the mourners of the greatness of God, even at times when they feel great sadness because their loved one has died.

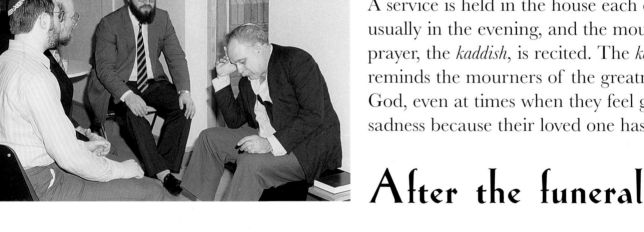

▲ *Jews believe that they are doing a good deed – a* mitzvah *– when they remember the person who has died and share the sadness of the mourner.*

After the funeral

At the end of one year, a simple gravestone is placed over the grave. There is a service by the graveside to mark this occasion. On the anniversary of the death, the person's name is read out during prayers in the synagogue. At home, the family will light a special candle, a *Yahrzeit* candle, which burns for 25 hours, to remember their loved one. They also say these words: 'As this light burns pure and clear, so may the thought of his/her goodness shine in my heart and strengthen me, Lord, to do your will. Amen.'

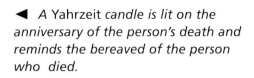

◀ A *Yahrzeit candle is lit on the anniversary of the person's death and reminds the bereaved of the person who died.*

It is a tradition that Jews name a baby after someone in the family who has died. Many children will be named after their grandfather or -mother or even great-grandfather or -mother. This tradition helps to keep memories of dead family members fresh in the minds of the younger generations.

What do Jews believe happens after death?

Some Jews believe that there will be a Day of Judgement when God will bring the dead back to life and judge all the good and bad deeds that they have done in the past. Jews believe that it is really important to follow the Commandments given to them by God, the *mitzvot*, throughout their lives. This is an obligation, like a contract that Jews have with God and must fulfil. They expect that good people will be rewarded in the next life, but they believe that they should concentrate on leading a good life on Earth, rather than trying to prepare for the next world.

Simon's story

'My name is Simon. I'm 14 years old. My mother told me that my grandfather had died when I came home from school. We went straight to my grandmother's house. My father had gathered the rest of the family there. The funeral was held the following day. I went with my father, my uncles and my older brother. Small tears were made in some of the mourners' jackets as a sign of their sadness. My mother stayed at home with my grandmother and aunts. The rabbi was kind to us all. He knew that we were upset that my grandfather had died. As the rabbi prayed, 'May his name be for a blessing', I thought of my grandfather, and although I was still sad, just remembering my grandfather's face, somehow made me feel better.'

The Hindu Tradition

What do Hindus believe about death?

Hindus do not believe that death is the end of life, but the start of a new life. So life is like a circle of birth, death and rebirth. Hindus believe that each person may have thousands of lives in this world and in each life a person has to do good rather than bad actions. When Hindus die, a part of them, their soul, or *atman* passes to a new life in another body. How they have lived in this and in previous lives will decide the kind of new life they will have next time. The result of good and bad actions is called karma. This rebirth in a new body is called reincarnation. Every Hindu wants this circle of birth, death and rebirth to end, because then his or her *atman* will be united with Brahman, the Supreme Spirit. This can only happen if people have good karma. Hindus believe that if they have good karma, they will be released from rebirth.

▲ *Brahman is the Hindu's Supreme Spirit. Hindus believe that everything begins and ends with Brahman.*

Sacred text

This sacred text tells Hindus that when people die it is no different from growing old and seeing your body change. When you die, your soul moves into a different body.

'Just as the dweller in this body passes through childhood, youth and old age, so at death he merely passes into another kind of body.'

(*Gita*: Chapter 2, Verse 13)

▲ *A body of a Hindu is covered with flowers and carried through the streets to the funeral pyre.*

What happens when someone dies?

In India, when a person dies, his or her body is cremated or burned. Usually this happens on the same day that the person dies. First the body is washed, if possible with water from the holy River Ganges in India, and sweet smelling sandalwood paste is rubbed all over it. Copper coins are placed over the eyes and then the body is wrapped in a white cloth and carried outside the town or village to a place where it will be cremated. A platform or funeral pyre is built from logs and sandalwood, which smells sweet as it burns. The body, often covered with saffron coloured flowers, is placed on this platform. Just as the bride and groom circle a fire at their wedding, so one of the dead person's sons walks round the funeral pyre seven times and then sets fire to the wood. A priest chants verses, such as the sacred text from the holy book, the *Gita*. Ghee or melted butter is poured over the body to help it burn. As the body burns, the dead person's skull cracks and at this moment Hindus believe that the soul or *atman* leaves the body.

15

Rajnee's story

'My name is Rajnee and I live in Ontario in Canada. Two years ago, my aunt died. My mum contacted all my aunts and uncles so that the whole family could come to the cremation. My aunt's body was washed and wrapped in a white sari because she was a widow. The body was then placed in a coffin. The cremation took place in the local crematorium. On the day of the cremation, a Hindu priest came to our house and chanted verses from the holy book, the *Gita*. One of the verses said: 'As a person leaves old clothes and puts on new ones, so the soul (the *atman*) leaves one body and enters a new one.' Then my aunt's body was burned and we collected the ashes. That summer, we all made a special trip to India and scattered the ashes on the River Ganges.'

After three days, the eldest or youngest son collects the ashes of the dead person and scatters them on a river. Hindus try to scatter the ashes on the River Ganges because they believe that the water of the Ganges can wash away a person's sins (bad deeds). Sometimes a Hindu who is very old or ill will go to the banks of the River Ganges to die, in the belief that this is the holiest of places.

▼ *The funeral ghats at Varanasi lead down to the holy River Ganges.*

▲ *Hindus gather together to mourn at the funeral of one of their community members.*

When someone dies, friends and relatives visit each day and bring food for the bereaved family to eat. After the funeral, family and friends mourn for 10 days. During this time, the family will not eat any sweet foods and men do not shave as a sign of respect and to signify their grief. Special foods such as rice balls and milk are offered to the family shrine. On the twelfth day, family and friends are invited for a special feast. Although the family will be sad that someone that they love has died, the Hindu holy book, the *Gita* teaches them that death is natural: 'Death is certain for the born. Rebirth is certain for the dead. You should not grieve for what is unavoidable'. *(Gita:* Chapter 2, Verse 7*)*

The Muslim Tradition

The journey of life

When a Muslim baby is born and the *Adhan,* or call to prayer, is whispered into its ear, the usual prayers that follow a call to prayer are not said. This is because the prayers for this particular *Adhan* are said in the mosque when that person dies. For Muslims, life is a journey which is completed at their death and the *Adhan* is completed too, as the final prayers are said.

▲ *People often visit the graveside of a loved one, to feel close to him or her – days, weeks or years after the funeral.*

Sacred text

Muslims believe that good people will go to Paradise to be with Allah. This text describes what Paradise is like:
'People who have faith and do righteous deeds are the best of creatures. Their reward is with Allah: they will live for ever in Gardens of Eternity beneath which rivers flow. Allah is well pleased with them, and they with Him: all this will be for people who love their Lord and Cherisher.'

The Qur'an: Surah 98: 7-8

When a Muslim is dying, he or she will try to say the *Shahadah,* the statement of faith in Allah. This shows devotion to Allah. When a Muslim hears that someone has died it is customary to say 'To Allah we belong and to Him is our return' (Qur'an: 2. 156). These words reinforce the idea that a Muslim is devoted to Allah and will be with Allah after death.

Like everyone, Muslims are sad when someone they care for dies, but Islam tells people to accept that death is part of Allah's will. It is said that even Prophet Muhammad (pbuh) wept when his son died. Muslims help and support each other. When someone dies, friends visit the bereaved family during the first few days to bring them food and to help them. The Qur'an is read regularly for 3-7 days to remind the family of Allah's comforting words in times of difficulty.

Prayers, led by a family member, are said at a graveside in Granada, Spain. ▼

Preparing for burial

Muslims believe in burying their dead and would never cremate a body because Allah decreed that man could not use fire to destroy what he has created. After death the dead person's body is usually prepared for burial by Muslims who knew and cared for him or her; this is seen as a final service which they can perform for the dead person. Women usually do this for women and men for men.

▲ *This Turkish-Muslim picture shows angels. Muslims believe that angels watch over the people of Islam constantly.*

Everyone, whether they are rich or poor, is treated the same when they die. The body is dressed in plain white cloth, three pieces for a man and five for a woman. These clothes may include their *Ihram* or *Hajj* robes which were worn when the person went on pilgrimage. The clothes may be made from cloth specially purchased in Makkah, the holy city of Islam where the Prophet Muhammad (pbuh) was born. The cloth is white to show that Muslims believe that to Allah everyone is equal.

A body is buried quickly, preferably within 24 hours, and if this is not possible, at the first opportunity. The body is taken to a mosque for prayers, often inside the prayer hall, which are usually led by close male relatives or friends.

The burial

The dead person is buried in a Muslim cemetery lying on his or her right side, facing Makkah. Muslims must turn towards Makkah when they pray, so they believe that even in death a person should look towards the holy city. The grave is built up with soil to remind people that this is a special place. At the *Id* festivals, such as *Id-ul-Fitr* which celebrates the end of *Ramadan* the month of fasting, Muslims often visit graves to show respect for the dead.

The Day of Judgement

Muslims believe that all through life two angels follow people around and record everything, good or bad, that they do. The angels are remembered every time that Muslims pray to show that the faithful know that they must behave well to reach Paradise. Muslims believe that after someone dies, an angel will ask a series of questions, and the way that these are answered will determine whether that person can be considered for entry to Paradise or not.

Muslims believe that the souls of the dead wait to go to Paradise. This will happen on the Day of Judgement, when the universe will be destroyed. On that day the dead will be resurrected to stand before Allah and be judged. Then the angels will give their records to Allah and everyone will be held responsible for how they have lived. Allah will decide who has been good enough to enter Paradise. Those that are rewarded with entry to Paradise will live there for all eternity in a state of great happiness. Very bad people will be sent to hell. Those that do believe in Allah but have sinned will be sent to hell for a short while until Allah allows them to enter Paradise.

◄ *This Muslim garden has a fountain, just as Paradise is said to have in the Qur'an.*

Maryam's story

'My name is Maryam and I live in Cairo. My mum died last autumn and I was really upset. My family came to look after me. We took mum's body to a nearby mosque to prepare it for burial. A lady there organized this with my aunt and some women friends. Mum went on the *Hajj* pilgrimage years ago, and so we used cloth that she had bought in Makkah especially to wrap her body for burial. The next day at the mosque I watched from the women's gallery as my dad and my uncle led the funeral prayers. I miss mum. Even if you have a religion of course you miss someone who has died, but, if it is Allah's will, we will meet again in Paradise.'

The Buddhist Tradition

What do Buddhists believe about death?

Buddhists believe that death is an inevitable part of life. Being born and dying are two of the many changes that happen to human beings and they are both quite natural. Buddhists remember how the Buddha learned an important lesson about life. Born a prince named Siddhartha, he had everything he wanted. However, on his journeys outside the palace, Prince Siddhartha saw an old man, a sick man and a dead man and learned that everyone grows old, can become sick and dies. He realized that unless people understood that all things are impermanent (do not last) they could never be really happy. Siddhartha became known as the Buddha or Enlightened One. He taught that in life each person should try not to cause harm to other creatures and should become aware of the way that all things are constantly changing.

This picture shows the Buddha's death. Just before he died, the Buddha said 'All ... things are of a nature to decay. Strive on untiringly.' ▼

Different beliefs about death

The ceremonies that take place when a Buddhist dies depend on the tradition and country in which the person has lived. Different Buddhist countries and different groups of Buddhists have different ways of marking death.

When a Buddhist dies, his or her family and friends will feel sadness and cry in their grief, and they know that it is natural to feel sadness at the loss of someone close. However, they believe that all life is about change. Dying is part of a natural and ongoing journey. Seeing the body of a person who has died is important for Buddhists. It reminds the family and friends that all of us will die one day, and this helps them to remember that they should live their lives well.

▲ *This funeral service was in South Korea, Asia.*

Life after death

Buddhists believe that when a person dies, he or she will have a new life to follow, and what kind of life it is will depend on how the person has lived before – whether he or she has been good or bad. This change from death to a new life is called rebirth or reincarnation. Through good actions people create their own happiness in this life and in lives to come. Living a greedy or spiteful life creates suffering and unhappiness, just as a generous and kind life creates present and future happiness. The Buddha taught: 'If with an impure mind a person speaks or acts, suffering follows him like the wheel that follows the foot of an ox.' (*Dharmapada* Ch.1 V1—2) All past actions are called karma and they determine your future. A person who has lived a good life will carry his or her good karma into the next life. Nirvana means ending the cycle of birth, death and new life. Some Buddhists believe that when someone is dying, it is important that they are reminded of the Buddha's teaching by reading sacred texts. If the person is too ill to do this, then Buddhist friends or monks will recite the scriptures to help them.

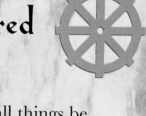

Sacred text

'May all things be happy and secure, may their hearts be wholesome. Whatever living beings there be – feeble or strong, long, stout or medium, short, small or large, seen or unseen, those dwelling far or near, those who are born and those who are to be born – may all beings, without exception, be happy minded.'

From the *Meditation of Loving Kindness*.

Preparing the body

After death, friends and relatives will wash the dead person's body. Once purified, the body may be put into a coffin or wrapped in material and surrounded with candles, flowers and incense. Sometimes the coffin is decorated with photographs and coloured lights. Often the funeral will not take place immediately, so that relatives from abroad can get to see the body and pay their last respects. During that period, monks will come to the house several times a day to chant from the Buddhist holy scriptures. The family of the deceased gives food to the monks which is also thought to increase the deceased's chances of a happy rebirth.

The funeral ceremonies

In some parts of Asia, the funeral ceremonies may last over 49 days, the first seven of which are the most important. Prayers are said every seven days for seven weeks and the head of the family should be present. Western families tend to have prayers said less regularly. Most of the funeral rites are carried out by monks, who chant *sutras* that will help the dead person, as well as saying prayers.

▲ At this Buddhist funeral rite, monks make offerings to the Buddha.

After a funeral, monks and family members may go to a shrine to meditate before the Buddha. ▶

The funeral

Many Buddhists prefer to be cremated because the Buddha himself was cremated. The night before the cremation, Buddhists may play music and everyone gathers together to eat. On the day of the funeral people go to the crematorium and mourners walk behind carrying flowers and incense. Monks may walk with the coffin, and chant *sutras*. Buddhists believe that the dead person's spirit will benefit from the words of the *sutras*. When they arrive at the cemetery, the coffin is placed on a funeral pyre. When the coffin has been burnt, the ashes are collected and may be kept in an urn.

Shanti's story

'My name is Shanti and I live in Cambridge, England. When my grandfather died, his body was dressed in his clothes, placed in a simple coffin and taken to the shrine room in the temple. For two days it stayed there surrounded by flowers and images of the Buddha. Many people came to pay their respects. They sat near the body and remembered that one day they too would die. On the day of the cremation, the body was taken to the crematorium. We all repeated the Three Jewels:
" I go to the Buddha as my Refuge
I go to the *Dharma* as my Refuge
I go to the *Sangha* as my Refuge"
These words reminded everyone that we should think of the Buddha and his teachings and these would help us at this sad time. Also being part of the Buddhist community, the *sangha*, would help us. As we all remembered my grandfather, the button was pressed to begin the burning of his body. A few days later, we went to the shrine room again to meditate. One of the monks chanted the *Karaniya metta sutta* (Meditation on Loving Kindness) which talks about loving kindness.'

The Sikh Tradition

The long sleep

Sacred text

This text tells Sikhs to behave well in this life, so that when they die they will be able to stay with God and escape reincarnation.

'Strive to seek that for which you have come into the world, find through the grace of the guru, God will dwell in your heart. You will abide in His presence, in comfort and in peace and not return ever to be born and to die once more.'

Guru Arjan Dev, from the *Sohila-Arti*.

Many Sikhs believe in reincarnation. They believe that death is the start of a long sleep for the soul, before it sets out on a new life. Each life teaches new lessons and brings a soul closer to God. Sikhs believe that souls are rewarded for good deeds and that when all lessons are learned God will free them from the need to experience another life. Then they will be able to join God and be liberated (*mukti*) from the cycle of birth and death. The Sikh holy book, the *Guru Granth Sahib*, says that this can only be achieved by living a God-conscious life, where everything you do is guided by the Word of God. Sikhs must try to avoid the evils of life.

Friends and family visit the deceased in his or her home before the funeral. ▶

What happens when a Sikh dies?

When a Sikh dies the evening prayer is said and everyone remembers God by saying '*Waheguru!*' meaning 'Wonderful Lord'. Everyone is treated equally in Sikhism because Sikhs believe that everyone is of equal importance and was created by one and the same God. So no matter how wealthy or powerful a Sikh may be in this life, his or her funeral will be the same as the poorest Sikh's. Sikhs believe in cremation, not burial, as the body that is left is just a shell for which the soul has no more use. The cremation should take place as soon as possible, and in India it usually happens on the same day as the death, or the next day.

▲ *A granthi reads from the Guru Granth Sahib at a funeral.*

Before the cremation, the body is washed. Traditionally yoghurt and water are used. It is then dressed in new clothes, including the Five Ks – the symbols of the Sikh faith: shorts, uncut hair, sword, bracelet and a comb. The body is then placed on a bier or in a coffin and covered with a plain cloth. It is brought home on the way to the funeral so that friends and relations can pay their respects to the dead person one last time. When a death occurs, the family and friends make arrangements to read the Sikh holy book, the *Guru Granth Sahib*. This can either be read whenever the bereaved wish or continuously (*Akhand Path*). The continuous reading takes approximately 48 hours to complete.

▲ *This Sikh watches as the cremation of a dead relative begins in a local crematorium.*

The funeral

On the way to the place where the cremation takes place, the body is taken to the *gurdwara* for prayers. It is not usually taken inside the building, the prayers are said outside the building. Then a procession takes the body to the funeral ground where it will be cremated.

Once they arrive, the friends and relations say a general prayer over the coffin. At a cremation site the funeral pyre is lit. This is usually done by the eldest son, or another close relation of the dead person. If the cremation takes place in a crematorium, the nearest relative will indicate when the cremation should begin. After the cremation, everyone returns to the *gurdwara* for the *bhog* service, in which *shabads* (hymns) from the *Guru Granth Sahib* are recited and sung.

Rupinder's story

'My name is Rupinder Singh. I was on holiday in India when my aunt died; we went to the Punjab for her funeral. Her body had already been prepared for her cremation. Then a huge procession of people appeared. They walked through the narrow streets of the town carrying her body, which was covered by a simple white cloth. When they got to the *gurdwara*, they stopped briefly for prayers before continuing to the cremation site just outside the town. A funeral platform was already prepared with sweet scented woods and incense. The body was cremated as we said prayers and sang hymns. Everyone was saying what a good woman my aunt had been and how badly she would be missed.'

Everyone shares *karah parshad*, a sweet which symbolizes equality of all humans, and then they have a meal in the community kitchen, or *langar*. Both of these rituals symbolize equality to Sikhs. They also remind everyone that life must go on for those left behind. Sikhs often give money to charity at this time.

Helping the family

After the cremation, friends visit the bereaved family for the next two weeks, to pay their respects and provide support. They talk together about the dead person, share happy memories about their lives with that person and help around the home. Sikhs believe that although everyone will miss the deceased, death is not sad. The dead person has learned the lessons he or she was meant to learn in this life and will move on nearer to God.

The final farewell

These Sikh ladies are preparing food for a langar *meal that will take place at the funeral of someone from the community.* ▼

In Sikhism it is forbidden to erect a tomb or memorial to a dead person because Sikhs do not believe that the body is of any use after the soul has left it. In India, therefore, after a cremation many families arrange for the dead person's ashes to be taken to Kiratpur near Anandpur Sahib. There they are sprinkled onto the waters of a river. Sikhs living outside India that cannot arrange to travel there for this purpose will still arrange for the ashes to be scattered onto flowing water in the local river or sea.

GLOSSARY

Adhan the Muslim call to prayer.

Akhand Path (Sikh) Continuous reading of the *Guru Granth Sahib* from beginning to end.

Allah the Islamic name for God in the Arabic language.

atman (Hindu) the Hindu soul – what makes a person individual.

bereaved people who outlive a friend or family member and can be said to have 'lost them'.

Brahman (Hindu) a Hindu god, the ultimate reality, the god from whom everything comes and to whom it ultimately goes.

crematorium a place where dead bodies are burned.

crucifixion a Roman form of execution used on criminals. They were nailed to a cross and left there to die.

deceased someone who has died.

eulogy a speech written to praise someone who is dead.

Five Ks the symbols of Sikhism worn by Sikhs, the names of which begin with the sound 'k' in Punjabi.

Gita the Hindu sacred text which was spoken by Krishna.

gurdwara (Sikh) Sikh place of worship.

Guru Granth Sahib the Sikh sacred text.

Hajj (Islam) annual pilgrimage to Makkah, which each Muslim should undertake at least once.

Id-ul-Fitr the celebration of breaking fast after *Ramadan*.

Ihram (Islam) a state or condition entered into to perform Hajj.

immortal when someone doesn't die and lives forever.

kaddish a Jewish prayer that is recited by mourners.

karah parshad (Sikh) sanctified food distributed at Sikh ceremonies.

karma (Buddhism) intentional actions that affect one's circumstances in this and future lives.

langar (Sikh) the *gurdwara* dining hall and the food served there.

Makkah (Islam) city where the Prophet Muhammad (pbuh) was born.

memorial something that helps people to remember a person, place or event.

moksha the final freedom, in Hinduism, from the cycle of birth, death and rebirth.

nirvana (Buddhism) state of perfect peace achieved when all life's lessons are learned and there is no need for any more lives.

Paradise (Islam) place of delight where Muslims will be with Allah after the Day of Judgement.

pbuh (Islam) literally 'peace and blessings of Allah upon him' used by Muslims every time the name of Prophet Muhammad (pbuh) is mentioned.

Prophet Muhammad the final prophet of Allah.

Qur'an the Islamic sacred text.

rabbi a Jewish teacher.

reincarnation (Hindu, Sikh) rebirth of the soul into a new life.

Shahadah (Islam) a declaration of faith.

sutra the words of the Buddha.

tallit (Judaism) prayer shawl.

tzizit (Judaism) the fringes on the corners of the *tallit*.

FURTHER INFORMATION

Books

Looking at Judaism: Special Occasions by Sharon Barron,
Wayland, 1998.
Religions Through Festivals: Buddhism by Peter and Holly Connolly,
Longman, 1989.
Hinduism by Dilip Kadodwala, Wayland, 1995.
Islam by Khadijah Knight, Wayland, 1995.
Sikhism by Kanwaljit Kaur-Singh, Wayland, 1995.
Islamic Festivals by Khadijah Knight, Heinemann, 1995.
Let's Talk about Death and Dying by Pete Saunders,
Watts, 1997

Websites

http://www.theresite.org.uk – An RE site that links to resources, organizations and agencies as well as containing research materials for children.
http://www.christianity.net/ – An extensive guide with stories, a church locator, and a database of over 9,000 Christian sites.
http://www.alsirat.com/silence/ – The web's most extensive cemetery site containing information about cemeteries, symbols, epitaphs, burials, tombstones etc.
http://www.sparksmag.com – An electronic magazine for Jewish youth, ages 9–13, with articles, interviews, polls and chat.
http://encarta.msn.com – This site contains information on Hindu beliefs and practices, including cremation.
http://www.hindunet.org – The Hindu Universe. This web site features a Hindu calendar, a glossary of terms and information on Hindu arts, customs, worship and scripture. Links to other Hindu resources are also included.
http://www.islam.org – IslamiCity in Cyberspace. An attractive site that explains about Islam and has a virtual mosque tour and a kids' page (http://www.islam.org/KidsCorner/Default.htm)
http://www.sikhs.org/ – An extensive range of topics, from teachings to ceremonies and festivals. Includes translated scriptures and contemporary articles.
education@clear-vision.org – The web site for the Clear Vision Trust, a project that provides Buddhist resources.

INDEX

All the numbers in **bold** refer to photographs